CHUBBY CHEEKS

Species Appropriate Hamster Care for Beginners

ALINA DARIA

ISBN: 9798583093366

Contents

Prologue

Hamsters are one of the most popular pets and enrich the lives of adults and children. They are cute, agile and interesting to watch. Nevertheless, many myths about hamster care still persist - and many accessories in pet shops are not species appropriate.

For the layperson, it can be difficult to separate correct from incorrect information. For most people, the pet shop is the first 'port of call' when it comes to buying hamsters and the advice that goes with it. Often, however, the advice given is wrong and the customer is advised to keep hamsters in a way that is very outdated and outmoded.

A hamster needs plenty of space to dig, run and explore. It needs species appropriate food that contains neither pellets nor vegetable by-products. They don't belong in a cage behind bars, they don't need to climb, but they do need plenty of bedding to dig extensively and to build their tunnels.

Many hamsters become very trusting in the course of time, they like to come out and let themselves be touched voluntarily. Other hamsters don't like to be too close or they need more time. Therefore, it is important to consider each hamster as an individual and to respect its wishes. After all, it is not a toy, but a living creature that can enrich our lives and that we want to take good care of.

However, don't blame yourself if you have made mistakes in hamster care so far. There is too much misinformation and dubious sources, so mistakes can easily happen. I've been keeping small animals for over 25 years and I don't even like to think about the mistakes I made when I started.

So, what do you have to consider when caring for hamsters? Let's get to the bottom of this question!

The best known and most popular hamsters

Cream gold hamster

The cream gold hamster belongs to the middle-sized hamsters and has its home mainly in Turkey and Syria. Its official name is *Mesocricetus auratus*. The fur structure and length does not differ from the original golden hamster, but the fur colour is different - the cream golden hamster has an even cream colour, usually resembling either ivory or apricot.

Rex gold hamster

The rex gold hamster has a protruding, curly or somewhat shaggy fur. However, it is not necessary to comb the hamster's fur. If necessary, a burrow box with maize granules can be offered, which will help to de-felt the hair even better.

Satin hamster

Satin hamsters can have different colours, but they share one common characteristic: Their fur is shiny and shimmering. The satin hamster can be either short or long haired. Its hairs are hollow inside - therefore light shines through the individual hairs, making them shimmer.

Dominant spot hamster

A dominant spot hamster has not only one, but several colours. These can range from black and white to beige and brown. There is still a myth that they tend to be more difficult to tame than other hamsters - but this is not true, as colour has nothing to do with a hamster's character.

Teddy bear hamster

Teddy hamsters got their name because of the longer and fuzzy fur, but they are simply Syrian golden hamsters with longer hair than other hamsters ("longhair"). The fur grows up to six centimetres long and often sticks out in different directions. This gives the plush impression. Children in particular could easily assume that they are like cuddly toys because of their appearance, however, it should also be noted with the teddy hamster that any expression of affection should be done in agreement with the animal.

Campbell dwarf hamster

A Campbell dwarf hamster has a narrow waist, a pointed head shape and relatively large ears. It has rather short fur and is one of the more trusting hamster species - although of course each animal has a very individual character. Campbell dwarf hamsters are the only hamster species that can be kept in a group under certain circumstances. However, this can only work if the Campbell hamsters are truly purebred and have never been mated with other species. This is very rarely the case, as many Campbell hamsters are mongrels. Keeping Campbell hamsters in groups should only be practised by very experienced keepers and breeders - all other Campbell friends are better advised to keep them individually. It should also be noted that Campbell dwarf hamsters - like all dwarf hamsters and hybrids - are at risk of diabetes. We will go into this in more detail at a later stage.

Chinese striped hamster

Chinese striped hamsters (*Cricetulus barabensis*) are far from the climbing skills of mice or rats but are considered the best climbers among hamster species. They owe this ability to their slightly longer tail and slender build. Animals can balance themselves by using their tails when climbing.

Djungarian dwarf hamster

Djungarian dwarf hamsters (*Phodopus sungorus*) are also rather trusting hamsters in most cases and are often easy to tame. Their fur is greyish/brownish, the belly is light, and they have a dark line on the back that runs over the entire body.

Roborovski dwarf hamster

Roborovski dwarf hamsters are small, compact and have short fur. Roborovskis are the smallest hamsters of all, but they are extremely active and even need a little more space than most other (dwarf) hamsters, as they are very active and lively. The colouring of the fur can vary: Many Roborovskis are piebald, some have white faces and others have completely white fur. The Roborovski's head is not pointed, but rather broad, and it has relatively large ears in relation to the body length.

Hybrids

A hybrid is a mix of two hamster species - a Djungarian dwarf hamster and a Campbell dwarf hamster. Hybrids are therefore not pure breeds. Mating should *only* ever be carried out by very experienced breeders, as significant diseases can occur if mating is done incorrectly. Hybrids can look very different, as the appearance changes depending on the colour proportions. Various unusual colours have been bred in the meantime - for example Russian Blue. Hybrids are extremely susceptible to developing diabetes, so they should always be fed a low-sugar diet!

© Kamila Lehn

Differences between Syrian gold hamsters and dwarf hamsters

Today we distinguish between large hamsters, medium-sized hamsters and dwarf hamsters. But which species belongs to which "size"? This we can remember very easily:

Large hamsters are not kept as pets - at least they shouldn't be. These are mainly the wild field hamsters. Unfortunately, these are now an endangered species, as field hamsters are often considered pests. They store up several kilos of food for the winter - five kilos and more are not uncommon. Field hamsters need this stockpile to survive, but logically grain farmers are not very enthusiastic about this. To prevent extinction, some field hamsters have already been placed under species protection. With a body length of up to 35 centimetres (13.8 inches) and a weight of up to half a kilogram (1.1 pounds), it rightly belongs to the large hamsters. It is not suitable as a pet.

For us, it is therefore only important to distinguish between medium-sized hamsters and dwarf hamsters.

Medium-sized hamsters mainly include the Syrian gold hamsters. With the dwarf hamsters it is even simpler because the name already gives the necessary information: All dwarf hamster species belong to the dwarfs.

The gold hamster species are more closely related to the wild field hamsters than the dwarf hamster species. With a body length of up to 15 centimetres (5.9 inches) and a weight of up to 200 grams (0.44 pounds), medium-sized/gold hamsters are quite a bit smaller than the wild large hamsters/field hamsters.

Dwarf hamsters are even smaller - they measure only up to eleven centimetres (4.3 inches) in body length and weigh up to 60 grams (0.13 pounds). Due to their smaller body size, they manage with somewhat less space than medium-sized hamsters; but the more space, the better!

Large hamsters	Medium-sized hamsters	Dwarf hamsters
Wild field hamsters	Syrian / gold hamsters	Dwarfs
Wild	Domesticated	Domesticated
Not suitable as a pet	Suitable as a pet	Suitable as a pet
Loners	Loners	Mainly solitary / loners (Campbells are an exception - only with animals of the same species, keeping them together requires special expertise!)
Up to 500 grams (1.1 pounds)	Up to 250 grams (0.55 pounds)	Up to 60 grams (0.13 pounds)
Up to 35 centimetres (13.78 inches)	Up to 15 centimetres (5.9 inches)	Up to 11 centimetres (4.33 inches)

Getting the hamster

Many people automatically associate the purchase of pets with the classic pet shop. However, the more information about pet shops spread, the more people distance themselves from the practices of pet shops. First of all, it should be remembered that pet shops are commercial enterprises that want to make a profit: Accordingly, pets are simply regarded as commodities in most pet shops. In many cases, the animals come from dubious breeders who 'produce' pets as mass goods and usually attach little importance to species appropriate breeding and caring. When one animal is sold, the next one is already waiting in line.

According to the German Pet Trade Association *(Zentralverband Zoologischer Fachbetriebe Deutschland e.V.)*, the pet industry generated a turnover of almost 4.66 billion (!) euros in 2016. With such large turnovers, one should be suspicious that the animals are regarded as mass-produced goods - similar to agricultural factory farming.

The animals rarely come from reputable breeders, but mostly from huge breeding facilities in which small animals vegetate. Due to the sheer mass of 'produced' animals, it is logically impossible to offer species appropriate care - most animals are hardly ever cleaned, sit in their excrements for days or weeks and have heaps of injuries and diseases that are not always recognisable at first glance. Cannibalism is unfortunately not uncommon in such breeding facilities either, as the animals are desperate, often get hardly any food, do not have enough space and dead animals are often not removed but left with their living conspecifics. Similarities to factory farming can also be seen here, as pigs, for example, are also prone to cannibalism when they reach the brink of desperation due to the conditions under which they are kept.

Most people rightly feel sorry for these animals and one might get the idea of wanting to save the animals from the pet shop. The idea is laudable and also understandable. However, one should keep in mind that one supports the mass animal trade when one buys an animal from the pet trade - even if only well-intentioned thoughts are behind it. Here, too, demand determines supply. If no one bought animals from the pet shop anymore, this 'business' would no longer be profitable, and the breeding industry would slowly die out. The mass pet trade would either cease altogether over time or the farms would have to massively improve their conditions to convince buyers to buy from the pet shop again. Every individual therefore has the power to determine the future fate of the animals - because the animals themselves cannot defend themselves.

So where can you get a pet from with a clear conscience? The first 'port of call' should ideally be animal shelters, hamster help centres or emergency stations. In these facilities you will find countless animals that have been abandoned by their previous owners or need help for some other reason. These animals usually did not have a good life and you get the chance to show a helpless creature how beautiful the world can be.

Another option for acquiring hamsters are reputable breeders. Here, a distinction must be made between 'breeders' and pure 'multipliers'. Serious breeders know their animals inside out. They usually have pedigrees that can even be used to trace the animals' grandparents or great-grandparents. Serious breeders are familiar with the genetics of the respective species, they keep the animals in a species-appropriate manner and do not make a profit. However, it should be noted here that the payment of a protective fee is perfectly normal. Through the protection fee, the breeder covers his expenses (or at least a part of them) and ensures that the animals do not end up as free snake food or the like. A serious breeder usually also wants to make sure that his animals are kept in a species appropriate way, which is why many breeders want to see the future enclosure in advance - this is not meant to be rude, but only shows that the breeder cares about his animals.

Multipliers, on the other hand, are usually not familiar with genetics and proper breeding. Many multipliers put males and females together at random and wait to see what happens. Often it is not possible to trace the origin of the previous generations or which diseases are inherited. It also often happens that males and females are not separated in time and pregnant females are acquired. Furthermore, breeders often give away the animals too early to get rid of them - but a hamster should not find a new home until it is at least six weeks old.

The hamster enclosure

For a long time, hamsters were kept in (small) cages - and unfortunately, many hamsters still have such a home today. In general, it can be said that the keeping of small animals has already improved massively in recent years, especially in German-speaking countries - the caring for guinea pigs and rabbits, for example, has also changed greatly for the better. Social networks and the internet in general have made a valuable contribution, as information can/could be widely disseminated. Unfortunately, however, there are no binding laws on the appropriate keeping of and caring for small animals - so many mistakes are still made, and outdated advice continues to circulate. If you too have kept your hamster incorrectly, don't blame yourself. When I was a kid, my first hamster lived in a relatively small cage and had a hamster ball to run around the house. That was almost twenty years ago.

© *Kamila Lehn*

Contrary to the widespread opinion that hamsters are good climbers, this is by no means the case. Hamsters are not good climbers, even though some try to. This is shown by the fact alone that they do not have a tail (or only a small stubby tail). Climbers balance themselves by using their tails - this is not only the case with cats, but also with rats or some species of monkeys. Hamsters, on the other hand, are burrowers. They dig underground tunnels, live largely underground and usually also bunker their supplies there. Many hamsters create real tunnel systems underground and it stresses them out if these tunnels are destroyed. There is a lot of work behind it. There is also the danger of hamsters hurting their little paws on the bars. Ideally, there should be no bars at all – but a fine grid is ok as a roof. Hamsters are also height-blind - this means that sometimes they simply drop because they cannot estimate heights. This can be very dangerous.

A hamster is therefore much better off in an aquarium or terrarium than in a cage. You will be given different information about the minimum size because there are no uniform regulations, especially none prescribed by law. However, nowadays there is an unwritten law that a hamster should be kept on at least 0.5 square metres (53 square feet) of floor space – an enclosure measuring 100 cm x 50 cm (approx. 40 inches x 20 inches) would be suitable, for example. These dimensions are also recommended by the Veterinary Association for Animal Welfare *(Tierärztliche Vereinigung für Tierschutz e.V.).*

Syrian gold hamsters, Chinese striped hamsters and Roborovskis need a little more space; for them, the enclosure should be at least 0.6 square metres (64 square feet). There is no upper limit - the more space your hamster has, the more comfortable it will be! Unfortunately, pet shops recommend cages with much less space and it is hard to find enclosures large enough in conventional pet shops. The height of the enclosure should be about 50 to 60 centimetres (19 to 24 inches) so that the air can circulate and there is enough space for a lot of bedding and furniture.

If you are on a budget, you may be able to find a suitable enclosure on the internet and buy it second-hand. It is important that you clean the used enclosure thoroughly, even if it appears to be clean. With second-hand enclosures, there is a regular risk of introducing either small pests or parasites that are not visible to the naked eye. Furthermore, it is possible that the enclosure still has the smell of the previous occupant - be it a hamster or another animal. At best, clean the entire enclosure with vinegar water first. Heat (at least 60°Celsius / 140°Fahrenheit) also kills parasites. You can and should do without chemical cleaning agents.

Of course, you can also build the enclosure yourself if you have some manual skills. With some wood and four plexiglass panes, you can create an inexpensive enclosure for your little friend.

Let's now move on to the equipment of the hamster enclosure and first look at the must-haves:

- sufficient bedding to dig in

- a house (ideally a multi-chambered house)

- a drinking bottle or bowl

- a sand bath

- a running wheel

- a variety of activities and hiding places

- nesting material

The bedding

It is very important that your hamster has enough bedding to dig in. In the past, many people made the mistake of only offering 2-3 centimetres (approx. 1 inch) of bedding. However, as the hamster is not a climber but a burrower and spends a lot of time underground, this deprived the hamsters of this opportunity. In fact, a hamster needs a scattering height of at least 20 centimetres (8 inches) throughout its enclosure - more is always better. Many hamster owners spread 30 centimetres (12 inches) or even more! This allows the hamster to build underground tunnels. Many hamsters build complex tunnel systems, which ideally should not be destroyed by humans, because this stresses a hamster a lot.

But don't worry: the bedding does not need to be changed regularly. If there are no illnesses - such as parasite infestation - it can even remain in the enclosure for the entire life of the hamster! You will only need to buy a lot of bedding at the beginning. Of course, you should clean the pee pits regularly and replace any leftover fresh food. If the animal dies, however, you should change all the bedding and clean the enclosure thoroughly before a new resident moves in. The smell of the previous hamster should not remain in the enclosure if a new hamster is to live there. Conventional small animal bedding is suitable. Hemp bedding is often recommended, but hemp bedding does not hold the tunnels very well. Furthermore, hemp bedding is quite hard, so it offers a greater risk of injury - for example, if the hard hemp bedding injures the hamster's eye.

Some hamster owners mix one third of the small animal bedding with hay. This is also in line with the recommendation of the Veterinary Association for Animal Welfare *(Tierärztliche Vereinigung für Tierschutz e.V.),* as it can make the bedding more borrowable. However, there are also many experienced hamster keepers who do without hay. If the bedding is well compressed, it is usually stable enough on its own to hold the burrows.

Important: Please note that all houses, the running wheel etc. should be placed on stilts that reach down to the ground! If the objects in the hamster enclosure merely remain loose on the bedding, there is a risk of collapse! If the hamster now digs its underground passages and these are built under loose objects, the passages can collapse and injure the hamster. In the worst case, the object itself will fall on its head or body - this can be fatal. Therefore, the hamster home must always be adequately secured.

© Katrin Specker

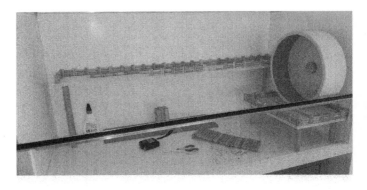

© Katrin Specker

© Katrin Specker

The house

The hamster will be happiest with a multi-chamber house. It should consist of at least two chambers - more chambers are gladly accepted. Hamsters are excellent 'sorters' and 'clean-uppers', because they like it tidy and always want to know what is in which place. There are a few hamsters that even clean up their own droppings and put them all in one place. Many hamsters also like to sort their food and separate the individual components from each other.

Ideally, the lid of the box should be removable so that it can be checked daily to see if any fresh food remains are rotting or if individual parts need to be cleaned in another way without destroying anything.

The food bowls (optional)

The fresh food should be separated from the grain food. If you want to use food bowls, you should therefore offer two different ones. Admittedly, many hamster keepers now do without food bowls altogether and instead distribute the food all over the enclosure. On the one hand, this keeps the hamster busy, as it has to find its own food - just like in nature - and is not presented with it all in one place. On the other hand, most hamsters have their own order anyway and put the food in the places where they think it is right.

Fresh food such as cucumbers and carrots should be cut into very small pieces. This will not cause it to rot, but in the worst case it will dry out. Rotten food can cause diarrhoea and even worse diseases, so it is important to check it regularly.

© *Kamila Lehn*

The drinking bottle or bowl

Both in terms of keeping hamsters and other small animals such as guinea pigs, rabbits and co. there is an age-old debate: which is better, drinking bottles or drinking bowls?

I personally only offer bowls and recommend this. At first glance, a drinking bottle may seem more hygienic as the water in the bottle does not come into contact with bedding, food or similar. However, in my experience, bowls are more hygienic than bottles as they are much easier to clean. A bowl is easy to rinse, you can reach all corners and cleaning with vinegar water is also very simple.

All bowls should be made of ceramic or a similar material to prevent chewing. Plastic bowls should be avoided - as should any other plastic material, as far as possible. Glass tea lights are also a good choice for bowls, as they are very small, and the hamster is therefore very unlikely to sit in the bowl.

In drinking bottles, on the other hand, all kinds of germs - and even algae - can form. Cleaning is more difficult, and you need a special brush to reach the corners.

Some hamster owners offer both options and first observe whether the hamster prefers a bottle or a bowl. In any case, the drinking place must be cleaned daily, and fresh water must be offered every day.

The sand bath

While running wheels are commonly known even by non-hamster owners, many people are not yet familiar with sand baths. However, they are essential for grooming the fur and claws. When a hamster rolls in the sand, the small grains of sand serve as kind of a brush.

The sand bath should be nice and big, so that there is enough space for extensive rooting around. A sand bath for a medium-sized hamster (Syrian hamster) should ideally have a diameter of 25 centimetres (10 inches), while for dwarf hamsters about 20 centimetres (8 inches) is sufficient. Again, bigger is always better.

With Roborovskis, it should be noted that they need more sand than other dwarf hamsters. With an enclosure size of 0.6 square metres, ideally one third of the enclosure should be divided off for the generous sand bath.

Many household items can be converted into a sand bath, so it does not necessarily have to be purchased separately. Some hamster owners, for example, use glass, ceramic or metal casserole dishes as sand baths. Again, please remember that all objects must be secured by stilts so that they cannot fall on your little friend's head.

Of course, you can also separate a certain part of the enclosure completely from the bedding and make this entire area available as a sand bath. In the sand bath itself, you can also provide your hamster with a small hiding place - for example, a small house made of ceramic or clay. This is often very popular.

The running wheel

Wheels are an often-debated topic in the hamster community. Due to the large number of defective wheels, a lot can be done wrong when buying. Please consider the following points before buying a wheel.

1. The wheel must be large enough, as small wheels stretch the back too much and this can cause health problems. The unnatural stretching of the back can cause posture problems and therefore lead to pain in the long run. For a dwarf hamster, the running wheel should have a diameter of 25 centimetres (10 inches), for a medium hamster at least 30 centimetres (12 inches). A wheel with an even larger diameter is also no problem.

For very small dwarf hamsters such as Roborovskis, wheels with a diameter of 20 centimetres (8 inches) may also be considered, but 25 centimetres (10 inches) is better even for the smallest dwarf hamsters!

© *Kamila Lehn*

2. The wheel should be made of wood. Coniferous wood is not suitable though because it may resin. I also find plastic less suitable, although many hamster owners use it, because plastic is easy to clean - e.g. if the hamster likes to urinate in the wheel.

With plastic, however, there is always the danger that the animal will chew on it and swallow plastic parts or injure its cheek pouches through the plastic parts. If your hamster doesn't pee in his wheel, natural materials should be preferred. In any case, metal wheels should be avoided, as they have been declared unfit for animal protection by the Veterinary Association for Animal Welfare for several reasons.

3. The wheel must not have any struts but should have a flat surface. It is sometimes mistakenly assumed that struts give the hamster a better grip on the wheel. However, this is a fallacy, as the hamster can easily injure its little paws on the struts. Unfortunately, this happens relatively often, especially when the hamster is running fast.

4. As with all other furnishings, the running wheel must be well secured, for example with stilts. It must not tip over or collapse when your hamster digs a tunnel under it.

5. One side of the wheel should be completely closed, the other side completely open. Grids, struts or other holes, including entry points, pose a risk of injury.

Please do not confuse running wheels with running plates. Running plates are not suitable for hamsters and pose a significant risk of injury. These plates are made rather for species such as chinchillas. The hamster can easily fly off a running plate and may be badly injured. In addition, hamsters do not have a straight posture (as with running wheels) when running on running plates - but run bent inwards. This sideways bending of the body can also cause health problems.

© *Saskia Schott*

Recreational activities and hiding places

The hamster should not get bored in his home. By digging the tunnels and collecting and sorting its food, the hamster can be well occupied, but in the long run this is not enough for many hamsters to have something to do all day or all night.

When hamsters are awake, they are very active animals and full of energy. They are very curious and love to discover new things. That's why many hamster owners offer their animals an additional run where they can let off steam.

Please make sure that all entrances and exits of your houses and activities are large enough so that the hamster does not have to squeeze through. You should also keep in mind that hamsters often have full cheek pouches, which make the hamster's head wider. Therefore, all entrances should have a diameter of at least seven centimetres (2.7 inches). For dwarf hamsters, five centimetres (2 inches) may be enough, but if you want to be sure, choose accessories with a larger diameter.

Houses and activities made of wood, cork or untreated cardboard can be offered. As with the wheel, you should avoid coniferous wood. Coniferous wood can resin and thus glue the cheek pouches. In addition, products made of coniferous wood are often stapled or nailed - this could injure the hamster. You can, of course, use materials you have gathered yourself, such as branches from hazelnut bushes, apple trees or other trees that are non-toxic to the hamster.

The following recreational activities can sweeten the everyday life for your hamster:

- willow bridges or other natural bridges (make sure, however, that the hamster cannot hurt himself on the grooves and close them if necessary)

- tubes and tunnels made of cork, wood or cardboard

- bottle boxes

- intelligence toys

- mazes

- food toys

Since hamsters are height-blind, you should avoid climbing facilities or furniture that is too high. A hamster cannot estimate the height, may fall and can injure himself. The height of the fall should not exceed 10 centimetres (4 inches) for dwarf hamsters and 15 centimetres (6 inches) for Syrian hamsters!

Nesting material

You can offer your hamster different materials for nesting. You can also first observe which material your hamster likes best and offer more of it.

Very popular is simple toilet paper as nesting material! This is cheap and most hamsters like it a lot. However, make sure that the toilet paper is not printed and not perfumed.

Furthermore, you can offer for example flax fibres/hemp fibres, paper flakes or also hay. If the hay is very long, you can cut it a little shorter at first.

However, you should do without the widely used 'hamster cotton', as it does not tear and could therefore cut off the limbs.

The hamster diet

Hamsters, like all pets, should be fed as species appropriate as possible. There are many similarities between dwarf and medium-sized hamsters, but also some differences.

Hamsters are omnivores. This means that they feed on both plant and animal food. Experience has shown that animal proteins, which the hamster body needs, are often neglected. The plant food components include various grains as well as fresh foods such as herbs, grasses, leaves, vegetables and in some cases some fruit. Regarding fruit, however, it should be mentioned right at the beginning that the dwarf hamsters bred nowadays are very susceptible to diabetic diseases and therefore should not be given any fruit at all. The same is true for the hybrids.

Unfortunately, most pet stores and other retail outlets currently do not sell species appropriate dry hamster food. Therefore, many hamster owners resort to online retailers. Hamster food from retail stores usually contains unhealthy pellets and vegetable by-products. This is a nicer euphemism for "waste". The vegetable waste left over from the production of other products is pressed for further recycling and added to pet food to make a profit on this as well. Furthermore, most retail feeds do not contain animal proteins such as mealworms. In addition, in most cases the mixing ratio is not optimal, as the dry food is often mixed with too many nuts and/or seeds such as sunflower seeds, which contain an extremely high number of calories and should therefore only be a treat.

The ingredients of the dry feed should be as natural as possible. As previously stated, in any case, avoid products with pellets and / or vegetable by-products. Even if the food contains sugar or honey, you should keep your hands off it. Too much sugar can cause significant harm to your hamster. Grains and seeds should be the main component of the food. A good food mixture contains healthy grains such as oats, rye, spelt, wheat, buckwheat, but also a small number of high-fat seeds such as sunflower seeds or hemp seeds. Legumes such as peas, lentils or chickpeas are also good and healthy components of a dry food.

As mentioned before, animal protein is unfortunately sometimes neglected, and some hamster owners are not aware that hamsters are omnivores. Therefore, the dry food should also contain dried insects such as mealworms - or you offer this separately. Living mealworms can be fed just as well. Furthermore, dried herbs or dried flowers are often found in species appropriate food mixtures. This is perfectly fine, but not a condition for a species appropriate food. Herbs and flowers can also be offered fresh.

Especially with dwarf hamsters you have to be careful that they don't take in too much sugar. They are very susceptible to diseases like diabetes. Dwarf hamsters do very well with millet, buckwheat and grass seed.

They also tolerate flaxseed and quinoa well. In addition, like medium hamsters, they also need animal protein, herbs and fresh food.

Once a day you should offer your hamster fresh food. It is best to cut the fresh food into very small pieces. This way it is more bite-sized for the little hamster and it will not go mouldy if the hamster buries it, it will just dry up. Nevertheless, it is recommended to regularly check if there is still old fresh food in the enclosure.

Similar to guinea pigs and rabbits, hamsters can meet most of their fluid needs by eating fresh food. Therefore, a hamster will usually drink less if it is given a lot of fresh food. It should be noted, however, that all of these pets have fairly sensitive digestive systems and therefore must be acclimated slowly to new foods. Otherwise, the digestive system can be thrown out of balance by too rapid a change and illnesses such as diarrhoea could result. The hamster should be accustomed to any new food slowly.

The following cabbage varieties can be fed, for example:

- Cauliflower

- Broccoli

- Kohlrabi (also the leaves!)

The following types of lettuce can be fed, for example:

- Chicory

- Iceberg lettuce (only small amounts, because iceberg lettuce contains hardly nutrients, but a lot of nitrate)

- Endive

- Lamb's lettuce

- Green/garden lettuce (also only small amounts due to the low nutrient density)

- Radicchio (extremely healthy)

- Romaine

The following tuberous vegetables can be fed, for example:

- Fennel

- Parsnip

Other vegetables that are good to feed:

- Cucumber

- Peppers (at best green peppers)

- Celery

- Spinach

- Tomatoes (although tomatoes are actually fruits; do not feed to hamsters with diabetes)

- Zucchini

Herbs and leaves:

- Basil

- Blackberry leaves

- Daisies

- Hazel leaves

- Chamomile

- Dandelion leaves and flowers

- Parsley (do not feed to pregnant animals, as it can induce labour pains)

- Peppermint

- Rose leaves

- Sage

Medium-sized hamsters (Syrian hamsters) may be offered some other fruits and veggies, which are not suitable for dwarf hamsters due to the increased sugar content. Dwarf hamsters have a higher risk of developing diabetes - therefore the following fresh food should only be offered to Syrian hamsters (in moderation and mainly as a treat!).

- Apple

- Pear

- Strawberry

- Raspberry

- Carrot

- Corn (fresh - not canned)

- Grape

The digestive system of the hamster

In this chapter we do not distinguish between dwarf hamsters and medium-sized/Syrian hamsters, as the digestive systems of the different species are the same. Hamsters are omnivores, so they need both plant and animal food.

The dentition resembles at first sight the dentition of other popular small animals (rabbits, guinea pigs), but here must be differentiated in some points. The incisors of the hamster are clearly visible, and it has two long incisors both above and below. These are sharp and are used to bite off pieces of food or to bite open seed coats. The hamster's incisors are constantly growing and must therefore be constantly worn down. In a species appropriate diet, this happens automatically and naturally through food intake. These teeth have no roots. The yellowish coloration of the incisors is normal.

© *Saskia Schott*

The molars, on the other hand, cannot be seen from the outside and are also difficult to check - this can usually only be done by a veterinarian. Unlike the incisors, the molars do not grow back steadily, but have long roots. Each hamster has six molars on the top and six on the bottom.

As with humans, the hamster's digestion begins in the mouth. The salivary glands make the food, which is crushed by the molars, smooth and 'slippery'; and the salivary enzymes begin digestion.

Hamsters are especially known for their cheek pouches. These are very stretchy and offer space for a lot of food. Hamsters often stuff their cheeks full to transport the food in here to their bunker. Adult animals can even stuff up to 20 grams of food into their cheek pouches and sometimes store or transport their entire food ration for the day in here.

Through the oesophagus, the chewed and ground food enters the stomach. However, it is important to distinguish that hamsters - unlike humans - have two stomachs. These two stomachs, although not clearly delineated from each other, perform different functions and should therefore be considered separately. They are the forestomach and the glandular stomach, which is often called the main stomach.

In the forestomach, the food is first soaked and stored before it is then transported further into the glandular stomach. In the glandular stomach, the food is now acidified, and the utilization of the proteins begins.

The hamster has a distinct stomach musculature, through which the food mash is mixed and always transported to the next station of the digestive tract with the help of the musculature.

This is another important difference from other popular pets such as guinea pigs or rabbits - they do not have such stomach muscles, but a "stuffing stomach". Therefore, rabbits and guinea pigs are always dependent on regular food supply and must not allow large pauses between eating, so that the newly supplied food pushes the already consumed food further into the next stations of the digestive tract - or simply "stuffs" it. This is not the case with hamsters.

In the small intestine, tissue water and various enzymes are now added to the pre-digested food, and the food components are broken down and further utilized. In the rear part of the small intestine, the nutrients are supplied to the hamster organism. This is followed by further processing in the large intestine, where the water is also removed from the food mush. In the rectum, the solid, hard droppings are finally formed before the hamster excretes them.

Typical behaviour of the hamster

Hamsters are flight animals, just like rabbits and guinea pigs. If there is a threat from enemies, loud noises or other frightening things, the hamster will take the precaution of quickly hiding in its burrow to avoid the danger and from there assess whether it can get back out into the open. However, if the burrow is too far away and there is no other safe place to hide, the hamster will either go on the attack and try to drive the enemy away by hissing - or play dead and appear frozen.

Hamsters, like guinea pigs and rabbits, are often attacked in the wild by birds of prey and grabbed from above. Even if a flight animal has been kept indoors its entire life and knows no natural enemies, the flight instinct is still ingrained in its instincts. Therefore, you should make sure to place the hamster enclosure elevated (and not directly on the ground), ideally at eye level or slightly lower. When you want to take your hamster out of the enclosure, your arm should approach from the side slowly and gently so that it doesn't resemble a bird of prey attacking from above.

Each hamster is individual and has its own unique character. Even though some hamsters are generally considered to be more trusting than others, each animal still has a mind of its own. Especially when acclimating a new hamster, it is important to give the animal as much time as it needs.

Some hamsters are not very skittish and are more adventurous; these animals may come to hand by the second or third day and rarely hide. Other animals need more time and patience; they may hide for days during the acclimation period and consider the human hand a threat.

Therefore, patience is essential during the acclimation process. The hamster should not be forced or coerced into anything but should be allowed to decide for itself how much closeness it will allow and at what pace.

When your hamster stands on its hind feet and looks around, everything is fine. He is surveying his surroundings, is awake and alert, but not unrelaxed. However, if he starts showing his teeth and raising his paws, he senses a threat. This is his way of warding off danger. Even if he puffs up his cheek pouches, screeches, growls or chatters with his teeth, this is a defensive posture to eliminate a danger and to threaten the opponent.

Relaxed hamsters yawn and stretch after sleeping. This behaviour is found in humans as well as in other animals. The mouth is opened wide when yawning and the paws are usually stretched out far forward. This is a sign of a relaxing sleep and that your hamster is comfortable.

© *Kamila Lehn*

Tendencies towards negative behaviours include excited squeaking, teething, or when your hamster moves around flat and crawls. Squeaking can be a sign of pain, crawling signals fear. Like many other animals, the hamster then tries to make itself as small and flat as possible to avoid being discovered.

Of course, biting is also a signal of negative feelings - the hamster is usually afraid and feels threatened. However, biting can also be a sign of pain and associated discomfort.

Many small animals - hamsters as well as guinea pigs and rabbits - gnaw on the bars of their cages. This is a sign of boredom and monotony in life. The hamster has nothing meaningful to do and can develop strange behaviours as a result, such as gnawing on the bars. This is another reason why hamsters should be kept in species-appropriate enclosures rather than in wire cages. If a hamster has enough bedding to dig in, enough things to do and plenty of space, it will usually not get bored.

Hamsters are very clean and tidy animals. Most hamsters have a designated pee corner. This, of course, makes cleaning easier. A few hamsters even re-sort their droppings if they are not happy with the tidiness. There are also many hamsters that sort their food - for example, sometimes the mixed dry food is meticulously separated and sorted according to the different ingredients. This is normal.

If possible, this order should also not be messed up - or not too much - as destroying its system can be extremely stressful for the hamster. The same applies to the tunnels the hamster digs underground. He has a special system here and does not like it when his hard work is destroyed.

Illnesses

In the following we want to talk about the diseases that occur most frequently in hamsters. In case of illness, always consult the veterinarian in charge. Your vet should be specialised in small pets.

Diarrhoea

Diarrhoea can have various causes. In hamsters, diarrhoea does not only occur when the droppings are watery, but also when the shape and/or consistency of the droppings change. Healthy droppings are evenly rounded and elongated or oval. The consistency is firm and almost dry.

Diarrhoea also weakens the animal, so that the hamster may appear tired, not be as active as before or take in less food and water. There may also be cloudy eyes and weight loss.

Diarrhoea should be taken very seriously and should be examined by a vet. Particularly if the hamster refuses water and food intake and if the diarrhoea lasts longer than a day, urgent action should be taken.

The most common causes of diarrhoea:

1. Too rapid a change of food - Any change of food should be done slowly. Do not offer your hamster too much of a new food at the beginning but increase the portions slowly. This is especially true for fresh food that the hamster has not yet experienced.

2. Mouldy food - For this reason, you should check your supply of dry food regularly to ensure that it does not show signs of mould. Mouldy fresh food should also be removed from the enclosure. Cutting the fresh food into very small pieces is a good way to prevent mould, as in the worst-case scenario the food will simply dry out.

3. Worm infestation or other parasites - Often small worms can already be seen on the faeces with the naked eye,

but the faeces should always be checked and analysed by a vet if a parasite infestation is suspected.

4. Poisonous plants or plastic parts - If the hamster comes into contact with poisonous plants in the home and gnaws on them, this can lead to symptoms of poisoning, often accompanied by diarrhoea. The same applies to gnawing on plastic parts.

5. Stress - If the hamster is exposed to stressful situations, it can cause enormous mental stress. A depressed mental state can affect physical health and often results in digestive problems - mostly diarrhoea.

Diabetes

Diabetes is unfortunately very common in hamsters. Dwarf hamsters in particular are at high risk of diabetes. It is sometimes difficult to recognise the disease. Signs of diabetes can be cloudy eyes, weight gain or very frequent urination. Even if the hamster drinks a lot, this can be a symptom of diabetes. In any case, this should be examined by a vet. In most cases, diabetes can be traced back to incorrect feeding methods, for example if a hamster eats too much sugar and fat. Therefore, especially dwarf hamsters should not be fed any fruit, and sugary vegetables should also be avoided.

Colds

Colds must be taken very seriously in hamsters. The hamster's small body is not as robust as the human body, for example, so a cold can very quickly cause dangerous pneumonia, which in the worst case can be fatal. A cold must therefore be counteracted very quickly, as the aggravation usually occurs much faster than in humans.

The symptoms are the same as in all mammals: Colds show themselves through sneezing, a runny nose, watery eyes, rattling breathing and similar cold symptoms. To avoid colds, draughts should be avoided. The hamster should also not be exposed to excessive temperature fluctuations. Nevertheless, always make sure that the hamster room is well ventilated. Stress or a lack of hygiene can also promote colds.

Cheek pocket injury or cheek pocket adhesion

The hamster's cheek pouches can stick together if it is offered food that is not of its kind - for example, sweets that are intended for humans. Fortunately, this does not happen too often. A bigger problem is furniture made of coniferous wood - in particular, many houses and running wheels are made of coniferous wood. This material can resin and thus also stick to the cheek pouches. Therefore, coniferous wood should be avoided. If the hamster sticks something sharp into the cheek pouch, it can be injured - this can also happen, for example, through small plastic parts. In any case, a vet should be consulted in the event of a cheek pouch injury or cheek pouch adhesion.

Fungal infection

If a hamster has a fungus, there are often round hairless areas on the body. The skin is usually scaly or has scabs. Fungus may also be accompanied by hair loss only - or scaly patches of skin may be found on hairless parts of the body such as the ears.

Fungal infections can be caused by poor hygiene and lack of air circulation, but many animals also suffer from fungal infections that have psychological causes. This can be due to too much stress, fear or other negative feelings, for example. A poor mental state also weakens the immune system, which can also cause fungal infections.

For the layperson, it is usually difficult to distinguish between a fungus, mites or similar. Therefore, a visit to the vet is indispensable. Please also note that a fungus is contagious and can be transmitted to humans as well as to other pets. Therefore, hygiene is also a top priority here.

Tumours

A tumour can occur even in the best cared for and happiest hamsters; even with the best health and excellent hygiene, it is possible for a hamster to develop a tumour. Therefore, prevention is extremely important. You should do a complete palpation of your hamster every now and then to look for hardened areas. If you discover an unusually hard spot under the skin or a small hard bump, you should visit the vet and have it checked out. The tumour may need to be surgically removed.

Abscesses

Abscesses can easily be mistaken for tumours, especially if the abscess feels hard. Unlike tumours, however, abscesses are collections of pus that are caused by bacteria. Similar to a tumour, an abscess can also occur in any part of the body. In most cases, abscesses are caused by external injuries such as bites or cuts on sharp objects, sharp branches or the like. Bacteria can enter the body through the open wound and possibly cause an infectious abscess. Even if the hamster scratches itself frequently and vigorously, an abscess can develop through these minor skin injuries. This is another reason why it is important to regularly palpate the hamster and look for hard or enlarged areas on the body. The vet will assess whether it is a tumour or an abscess. Not all abscesses need to be treated surgically, this is always a case-by-case decision. In any case, it is important that the pus is drained properly so that the abscess does not burst and possibly cause blood poisoning.

Parasite infestation

Hamsters can be infested by many different parasites. The most common parasites are fleas, hair lice, grain weevils, mites, moths and dust bunnies. The exact type of parasite can sometimes be very difficult to determine by a layperson, so the vet is essential here too. However, in order not to stress the hamster too much, you don't necessarily have to take it to the vet immediately - unless it is suffering noticeably from the infestation and already has health complaints. If the hamster is doing well, you can first fix a few of the pests on a piece of tape and then take this to the vet so that he can first determine the exact type of parasite. Be careful not to squash them so that the vet can examine them properly.

Usually, after a parasite infestation, the entire enclosure must be cleaned, the bedding replaced, and the furniture heated out to get rid of the pests completely. In case of an infestation with dust bunnies or demodex mites, however, a complete cleaning of the enclosure is not necessary, as the stress caused by the cleaning weakens the hamster's immune system even more and the parasites can multiply even more as a result. But again, please discuss this with your vet.

Epilogue

I hope that this guide has helped you. As we have seen, the hamster is a very special creature and differs greatly from humans and other small animal species. It is therefore important to know what the hamster's needs are so that they can be catered for in the best possible way.

If you have any further questions, please feel free to contact me by email. You can find my email address in the legal notice at the end of this guide.

Finally, dear reader: Product reviews are the basis for the success of authors. Especially independent authors depend on reviews from their readers. Therefore, I would be grateful for a review of this book. Please let me know in your review how you liked the book. This will also help future readers and earn you some points on your karma account! Thank you very much.

I wish you lots of fun and joy with your hamster, all the best and stay healthy!

Legal Notice

Author: Alina Daria Djavidrad

Contact: Wiesenstr. 6, 45964 Gladbeck, Germany.

E-mail: info@simple-logic.net

Web: https://www.simple-logic.net

Printed in Great Britain
by Amazon